How can I deal with...

When People Die

Sally Hewitt

W
FRANKLIN WATTS
LONDON • SYDNEY

First published in 2007 by Franklin Watts

Copyright © Franklin Watts 2007

Franklin Watts
338 Euston Road
London NW1 3BH

Franklin Watts Australia
Level 17/207 Kent Street
Sydney, NSW 2000

Series editor: Sarah Peutrill
Art director: Jonathan Hair
Design: Susi Martin
Picture research: Diana Morris
Series advisor: Sharon Lunney

A CIP catalogue record for this book is
available from the British Library.

Dewey no: 306.9
ISBN: 978 0 7496 7090 0
Printed in China

Franklin Watts is a division of
Hachette Children's Books, an
Hachette Livre UK company.

Picture credits:
Andy Crawford: front cover inset, title
page, 9, 10
Caro/Topfoto: 19, 20.
Bob Daemmrich/Image Work/Topfoto: 28.
©Esbin-Anderson/Image Works/Topfoto: 6.
Willie Hill, Jr./Image Works/Topfoto: 11.
James Marshall/Image Works/Topfoto: 22.
Brian Mitchell/Photofusion: front cover
main.
Network Productions/Image
Works/Topfoto: 7.
John Powelll/Topfoto: 5.
Nancy Richmond/Image Works/Topfoto: 4.
Ray Roberts/Topfoto: 27.
Ellen Senisi/Image Works/Topfoto: 8, 12, 13,
15, 21, 23, 24, 25, 26.
Skjold Photographs/Image Works/
Topfoto: 18.
Jim West/Image Works/Topfoto: 16, 17.
Every attempt has been made to clear
copyright. Should there be any
inadvertent omission please apply to the
publisher for rectification.

**Please note: Some of the photos in
this book are posed by models. All
characters, situations and stories are
fictitious. Any resemblance to real
persons, living or dead, is purely
coincidental.**

Contents

I don't know what's happening!

Lola's granny has died but her family haven't told her yet. They stop talking when she comes in the room. Lola feels worried and afraid.

Ewan is Lola's big brother

Lola keeps asking me, "Where's Granny? What's happened?"

I want to tell her, but Mum and Dad say

Lola's too young to understand about Granny dying.

But not knowing is making Lola feel unhappy.

Lola's story

Granny was staying with us because she was ill. Mum was looking after her. One evening, there was lots of running about, whispering and phone calls. No one would tell me what was happening. Mum asked me to stay in my bedroom.

I saw an ambulance from my bedroom window. They took Granny away. Mum says Granny isn't coming back, but she won't tell me why. What's happened to Granny? Are they whispering because they don't want me to know that Granny doesn't love us any more?

What can Lola do?

Lola is worrying because she doesn't know what's happened to her granny.
She can:

✔ tell her mum she is worried
✔ ask why Granny has gone away
✔ say not knowing is making her think frightening things.

What Lola did

I told Mum I thought Granny wasn't coming back because she didn't love us. So Mum gave me a hug and told me Granny had died. I burst into tears because I'll never see Granny again. Mum said Granny loved us and her love will never leave us.

I feel a bit better but I wish Granny was still here.

Granny's 70th birthday

What is death?

Death is when someone's body stops working and can't be made better.

Death is a natural part of life. All living things – plants, animals and people – grow older and eventually die one day. Living things don't live forever.

People die because their body gets old and worn out. They die because they are too ill to get better. Sometimes people die because they have a very bad accident.

A dead body can't feel pain or know what's going on.

I don't want to say goodbye!

Tim finds it hard to believe his dad has died. He won't go to the funeral to say goodbye because he wants to think he will see his dad again.

George is Tim's friend

I know Tim's dad has died, but he keeps talking about him as if he is still alive.

He got really cross with me when I said I was sorry about his dad.

Tim's story

Dad hasn't been well for ages. He's had medicine and operations and they've always made him feel better! But Mum says that Dad got too ill for the medicine to work any more. She says Dad died.

I can't believe Dad died. I think, if I don't say goodbye to Dad and if I don't go to the funeral, he'll walk in the door again, smiling! I'm afraid if I say goodbye I really will never see him again.

What can Tim do?

It would help Tim to know that he won't see his dad again. He can:

✔ talk to his mum about it and listen to what she says

✔ go to his dad's funeral and say goodbye

✔ write a goodbye letter to his dad.

What Tim did

I told Mum I didn't want Dad to be dead! We both cried together. Mum said I could write Dad a letter. She said people who loved Dad would be at his funeral. We would all remember him and say goodbye. I'm going to the funeral. It helps to think I won't be the only one saying goodbye.

What happens at a funeral?

The body of the dead person is put in a wooden box called a coffin. Their body is either buried, which means put in the ground, or it is cremated, which means burned. Their name is written on a gravestone, a plaque or in a special book of remembrance.

Family and friends of the person who has died get together to remember them and say goodbye.

A religious service or ceremony may be held.

I'm angry with my brother for leaving me

Wes's older brother Denny died in an accident. Wes feels angry with his brother for leaving him on his own and making his mum and dad unhappy.

Ricky is Wes's friend

Since Denny died, Wes is angry all the time – with Denny for dying and with his mum and dad about everything! He gets really angry if I talk about my big brother. I can't say anything right!

Wes's story

A car knocked my big brother Denny off his bike and hurt him so badly he died.

I'm angry with Denny. I keep thinking he should have been more careful!

Now Mum and Dad are sad all the time. I can't talk about Denny because it makes them even sadder.

And they worry about me. They keep saying, "Be careful Wes!" They won't let me ride my bike.

My friend Ricky's big brother is alive but mine is dead. It's not fair!

What can Wes do?

Wes's mum and dad feel sad and worried because of Denny's accident. Wes can talk to a grown-up he trusts. He can:

✔ say he feels angry with Denny

✔ say he knows his mum and dad worry about him

✔ say he doesn't like it when they think he is going to have an accident too.

What Wes did

I talked to Uncle Pete and he talked to Mum and Dad. Now they let me ride my bike in the park. I'm taking a cycling test so I can be safer when I ride on the road.

But I think Mum and Dad will always worry about me more because of what happened to Denny.

Will I ever stop feeling sad?

Vikki's mum died a year ago but she often feels sad. She wonders if she will ever be happy again.

Jay is Vikki's friend

Sometimes when Vikki and I are having fun and she's laughing and happy, she suddenly gets sad and won't play any more. I know she's thinking about her mum but she won't talk about it.

Vikki's story

On Wednesday it's the anniversary of Mum's death. It's a whole year since she died, but I still feel sad.

Every time I do something I used to do with Mum, I miss her and feel like crying because she isn't here any more. I cried when Dad helped me make my birthday cake because Mum and I always did it together. Dad cried too.

Sometimes I forget that Mum died and I feel happy. Then I remember and I feel sad again.

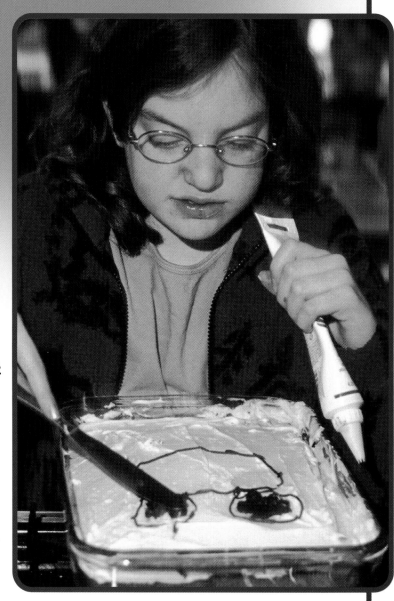

What can Vikki do?

Vikki will always miss her mum. It helps to have happy memories. She can:

✔ tell her friend Jay how she feels

✔ talk to her dad

✔ plan to do something on the anniversary of her mum's death so that it isn't just a sad day.

What Vikki did

I talked to Dad and he said he still feels sad too. We decided to make Wednesday a special day for Mum. We cooked her favourite meal, went on her favourite walk and even told her favourite jokes! We'll always be sad that Mum died, but we don't always have to be sad when we remember her.

I'm afraid I will die too

Luke thought that only pets and very old people died. So when his friend Sid died he was shocked. Now Luke is afraid of dying too.

Amos is Luke's friend

Luke and Sid were my best friends. Sid died because he was very ill. Now Luke thinks he's going to die too. But just because Sid died, it doesn't mean Luke or I are going to die.

Luke's story

I was sad when my pet hamster died and I cried when Nan died. But I didn't worry because hamsters don't live for very long and Nan was very old.

Then Sid died. He was only a kid like me! Now I think about dying all the time. I worry that Mum and Dad will die. I worry that I will die.

I can't get to sleep. When I do, I have nightmares. I go into Mum and Dad's room to make sure they are okay.

Amos keeps saying, "Of course you won't die!" He gets fed up with me. I don't want to tell Mum and Dad in case they get fed up with me, too. I wish I didn't feel so afraid.

What can Luke do?

Worrying about dying is making Luke unhappy.
He can:

✔ tell his mum and dad he is afraid of dying

✔ say he is afraid they will die.

What Luke did

I told Mum and Dad. They said everyone has to die sometime, but there was no reason to think

any of us would die soon. They said I must tell them when I feel afraid. But I don't feel so afraid now I've talked to them. I do miss Sid though.

My parents don't love me now

Nesta's mum and dad are sad that baby Sheri died. Nesta thinks they loved baby Sheri more than they love her.

Deena is Nesta's friend

Nesta told me her mum and dad talk about Sheri all the time. She thinks they wish she had died and not Sheri. She tries to be good so they will love her more. But I said, "Our mums and dads love us when we're good and when we're bad."

Nesta's story

Sheri died when she was only a baby. Mum and Dad talk about how sweet and good she was. They say, "Sheri would have been a lovely girl."

I'm not sweet and good all the time. Sometimes I'm naughty. So I think Mum and Dad wish Sheri was alive instead of me.

I try to be good so they'll love me and be glad I didn't die. Sometimes, I feel angry with Sheri. I feel bad about that.

What can Nesta do?

She can:

✔ Remember - her mum and dad love her and they would be very sad if she died

✔ Tell her mum and dad how she feels.

What Nesta did

I told Mum and Dad I thought they wished it was me, not Sheri who died. I said I would try to be good. They gave me a big hug and said they loved me all the time – even when I was naughty.

Now I know they love me, I'm not angry with Sheri any more.

I miss granddad too

Brendan thinks no one knows how much he misses his granddad. Brendan's granddad was very popular with his family as well as his friends. They are all sad he died but Brendan is very sad, too.

Ali is Brendan's friend

I know Brendan really misses his granddad. His mum, dad, aunts and uncles all help each other when they feel sad. I try to help Brendan when he feels sad.

Brendan's story

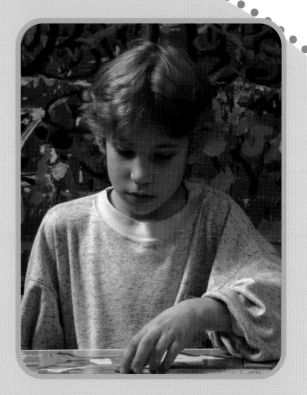

Granddad was my dad's father. Everyone loved him. He had lots of stories to tell and he was kind and funny. He called me his "little pal" and we did things together.

When he died, everyone was sad – Dad, Mum, my uncles and aunts and Granddad's friends. When they get together to remember Granddad, I feel left out.

I miss Granddad just as much as they do.

I'm afraid if I talk to Dad or Mum about Granddad, it will make them sad all over again.

What can Brendan do?

He can:
- ✔ talk to his friend Ali
- ✔ talk to his aunts or uncles
- ✔ tell them he misses his granddad and that he feels left out.

What Brendan did

I talked to Ali. He said the grown-ups would understand that I missed Granddad too. So I talked to Granddad's sister. She is making a book with photographs and letters and stories about Granddad, and I'm helping her. We put something new in the book when we feel sad about Granddad and it helps us feel a bit better.

How can I remember someone special?

Someone who has died can always be part of you. Remember:

✔ special things they did and said

✔ happy times together

✔ games and jokes you shared

✔ books and television programmes you both enjoyed.

You could also:

✔ make a photo album

✔ make a box of memories. Put in things such as a card they sent to you, a scarf they wore or their favourite poem

✔ help to raise money for charity in their memory

✔ plant a tree for them and watch it grow.

When our friend died

When Caitlin and Scott's friend Ruby died, they were shocked and very sad.

Caitlin: When our dog Sandy died, I was really sad that I wouldn't see him again. I never thought the same could happen to one of my friends.

Scott: When Ruby died, I was really shocked. I thought only old people died.

Caitlin: Scott and I were Ruby's best friends. Ruby's mum and dad asked if we wanted to go to Ruby's funeral. I wasn't sure. I'd never been to a funeral.

Scott: Ruby asked me if I wanted to go. I wasn't sure either, but I'm really glad we went.

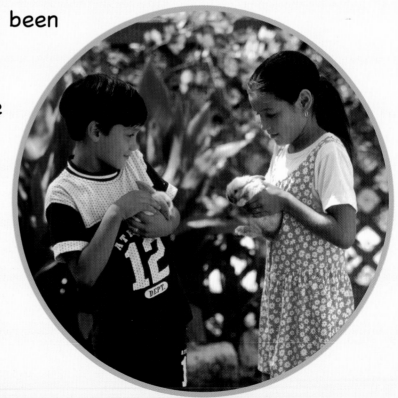

Caitlin: At Ruby's funeral, her mum and dad, her big brother and our teacher all talked about Ruby and how special she was.

Scott: All the children in our class wrote something for Ruby. There were letters, poems, stories and even jokes.

Caitlin: Her mum and dad read some of them aloud at the funeral. Then they put them with the flowers and cards people had sent.

Scott: Ruby's mum and dad said they were very pleased we had come to the funeral.

Caitlin: I felt really sad when I got home and I cried. Mum gave me a hug and said I would begin to feel better but it might take a long time.

Scott: At school, we planted a tree for Ruby. I think about her every time I see it.

Caitlin: Now we don't feel sad about Ruby all the time. We are often happy and have fun but it doesn't mean that we have forgotten Ruby.

Glossary

Accident
Something that happens suddenly and unexpectedly. Some very bad accidents can hurt or even kill people.

Afraid
You are afraid when you feel worried about something bad happening.

Alive
People, plants and animals are all alive. When you are alive you move, eat, sleep, learn and grow.

Ambulance
A van with special equipment that carries people to and from hospital.

Anniversary
An anniversary is when you remember something that happened on the same date every year. Your birthday is the anniversary of the day you were born.

Die
When someone dies, they are not alive any more.

Funeral
A funeral takes place when somebody dies and their body is buried or cremated.

Miss
You miss someone when you feel sad that you don't see them any more.

Sad
You are sad when you feel unhappy. When you feel sad you sometimes want to cry.

Worry
You worry when you don't know what is going to happen and you think something bad might happen.

Further information

For children

www.kidshealth.org/kid/
feeling/emotion/somedie.html
Learn about what happens
when someone dies and how
to deal with feelings.

www.childbereavement.org.
uk/youngpeople
Support and advice for
young people when someone
dies.

www.rd4u.org.uk
A website designed for
young people by young
people. The website supports
people after the death of
someone close.

www.winstonswish.org.uk
[Click on 'Young people']
An adult-free zone! It's just
for young people like you,
who know exactly what it is
like to have someone
important to them die.

In Australia

www.kidshelp.com.au
Tel: 1800 55 1800
Kidshelp is the free helpline
for children in Australia.
You can talk to someone
about any problem.

For adults

www.winstonswish.org.uk
Help for grieving children
and their families.

www.crusebereavementcare.
org.uk
Cruse Bereavement Care
exists to promote the well-
being of bereaved people and
to enable anyone bereaved
by death to understand their
grief and cope with loss.

www.bbc.co.uk/relationships/
coping_with_grief/
bereavement_index.shtml
Information on the
experience of bereavement.

Note to parents and teachers: Every effort has been made by the Publishers to ensure that
these websites are suitable for children, that they are of the highest educational value, and
that they contain no inappropriate or offensive material. However, because of the nature
of the Internet, it is impossible to guarantee that the contents of these sites will not be
altered. We strongly advise that Internet access is supervised by a responsible adult.

Index

Notes for parents, carers and teachers

Children can feel sad and confused when someone they love dies. They often don't really understand what has happened. There are many ways that adults can help children deal with their grief.

• Children need to know what has happened and that the person who has died will not come back.
• Being able to express thoughts and feelings is an important part of dealing with grief.
• Questions, doubts and fears should always be taken seriously.
• It helps children to share happy memories of the person who has died.

Page 4 Lola's story
Lola's parents think she is too young to be told her granny has died. She thinks Granny has gone away because she doesn't love her any more.
• Children need to be told plainly what has happened – that Granny has died – not that she is asleep or gone away.

Page 8 Tim's story
Tim doesn't want to go to his dad's funeral. He won't face the fact he'll never see his dad again.
• A funeral gives children a chance to share grief and happy memories with other people. Saying goodbye can help them to accept what has happened.

Page 12 Wes's story
When Wes's big brother was killed in a road accident, Wes was angry with his parents for worrying about him.
• It helps parents to remember that their grief over the death of a child can affect how they act towards their other children.

Page 15 Vikki's story
Vikki is worried she will never stop feeling sad about her mother's death.
• An anniversary of someone's death can be turned into an opportunity to share happy memories of them.

Page 18 Luke's story
Ever since his friend died, Luke has been worried about dying.
• Children need to know that everyone dies eventually. Understanding that early death is unlikely can help them to overcome fears and get on with normal life.

Page 21 Nesta's story
Nesta is unhappy because she thinks her parents wish she had died, not her baby sister.
• Children need to know that they are special and that their parents love them for who they are.

Page 24 Brendan's story
Brendan doesn't want to upset his parents by telling them how much he misses his granddad.
• Another member of the family or a friend can sometimes help a child with their grief if the parents are too sad themselves.

Page 28 Playscript, Caitlin and Scott's story
Children could 'perform' the parts in this simple playscript and then discuss what happened.